MW01641604

ISBN-13: 979-8-9913281-0-4

Published by: Arbuckle Art & Design — Scott Arbuckle

Website: ThadAndHarvey.org
Original story, characters, and illustrations by Scott Arbuckle.
Digital production and editing by Greg Parke.

To my wife, Tammy
who has helped me
build so many things in life.

And thanks to my long-time
friend and fellow book-lover, Allen
Arnold, for his encouragement
and coaching over the years.

Why?

We live in a world saturated with video screens, virtual experiences, and push-button play. All those things have their place. But I wonder what we are losing as hands-on activities, and imagination-driven learning are increasingly driven out of childhood?

I remember the joy of childhood as turning my mind loose, on a day when I could be on any adventure my mind could create. This is a book about sharing that.

What it's NOT.

This is not a "How-To Build a Tent."

If it helps a kid do that, then great. But the steps outlined in this book are just a suggestion.

What I REALLY hope this book will be, is a jump-start to a world of hands-on, problem-solving and imaginative improvisation. Its more about the process than about getting it right.

Hi.

I'm Thad. This is Harvey. We call ourselves, "Backyard Builders."

I guess we got started when I was younger,....and at home without much to do.

On one of those days, Harvey looked at me. And I knew what he was thinking.

"Can't we do better than this?!"

I was tired of all my usual toys. All they let me do was push a button, or stare at a screen.

I looked at all the stuff in the recycling bin, and wondered at what could be done with it. I recalled a story my Dad read to me called “Robinson Crusoe”.

It was about this guy who gets stuck on an island, all by himself. He has to figure out how to get along with just the junk he could find.

As I remembered that story, all the junk went from looking like this...

...to looking like THIS!

Harvey and I were getting excited!
We took all of our loot out into the backyard and started thinking about what we could do with it.

We were no longer "bored-to-tears" Summer prisoners. We were now locked into a battle for survival on a deserted island.

What could we do with the stuff we had at hand?

The first thought we had was,...
"We gotta escape this island!!!"

So we started figuring out how to make a boat that we could sail home on.

About that time, my sister came to see what we were up to.

She said that a boat sounded like a bad idea... we would probably sink and be eaten by sharks.

"Besides," she said. "Wouldn't it be more fun to live on the island?" "What you need is a house!".

So, Harvey and I took a long look around our island (the backyard). Maybe we can do something with this old tree... and even the rusty swing set we had outgrown.

But before we got started, we remembered that we were on a deserted island with no doctors. So, we had to be SAFE!... goggles,... AND,... no sharp tools (until Mom or Dad got home).

Then, I had an idea of how to use the old tree.
I got a water bottle, some twine, and an old bed sheet.
Harvey looked worried.

Harvey did not get my idea at first. But when he did,...
he got really excited!

*see pages 26 & 27 for more detail

We knew we weren't supposed to be using any sharp tools unless we had help, so we figured out ways to tie the sheet down without cutting or poking anything. It also meant, that if we changed our minds, we could use the sheet in other ways.

Besides water bottles, buckets full of sand from the old sandbox were good ways to hold down the rope from corners of the sheets.

An old tennis ball or golf ball made a good thing to hold the sheet to the rope.

We had our own island, and our own hut,...but about that time, we started wondering what we would do when we got hungry?

It's a good thing my sister floated by about that time.

"Mom says it's time for dinner," she announced.

Some more to chat about:

The structure that Thad and Harvey built was scrounged up from typical residential garage junk, but it actually has some interesting architectural heritage.

What they had fun building on a summer afternoon, is very similar to some of the earliest human efforts at architecture.

The Yurt of Asia, and the Tipi of the North American natives of the Great Plains, rely on the same tensile structural properties.

In more recent history, the circus tents of the early 1900's, and the modern airports, in places like Denver, use fabric structures held in tension by cables.

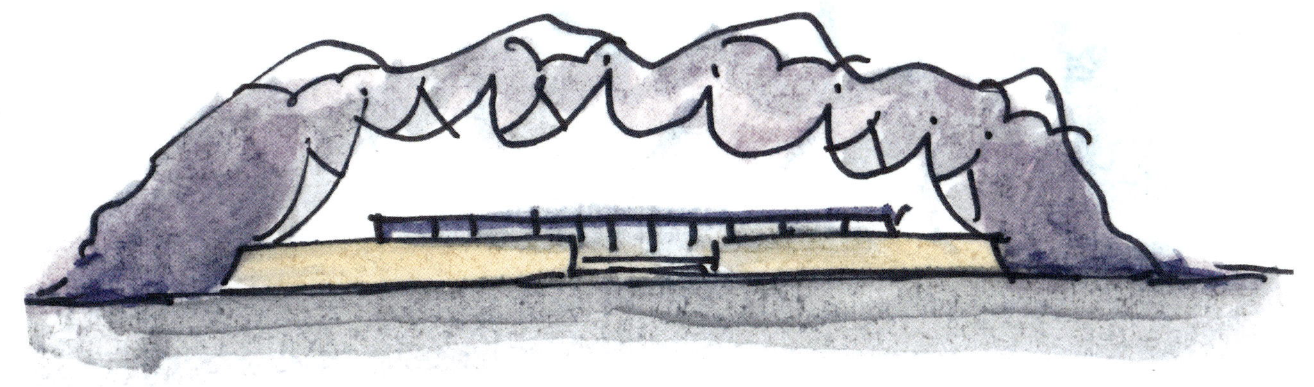

Scott Arbuckle
Creative Director

Scott Arbuckle is an architect and illustrator living in Carrollton, Texas. He has illustrated children's books about the life of Jesus, and Texas history. He is also the writer and illustrator of, **Zeb! The Cow's on the Roof Again!**

He has made a large part of his architecture career, designing branded environments like retail stores, and restaurants. He has remained a hand-drawing designer and illustrator since his graduation from Texas Tech in 1983.

One of the things he has found fascinating about buildings, both humble and grand, is that every building has a story to tell.

He is married to Tammy Fisher Arbuckle, and they have two grown children, and seven grandchildren.

Some Suggested Steps (feel free to improvise)

Lay out the sheet and locate the center.

Place the tennis ball in the middle.

Tie the rope around the tennis ball inside the sheet.

Get some weights to hold down the corners. Water bottles, or buckets of sand work.

Attach one of the water bottles to the rope from the center of the sheet.

Toss the bottle over a limb without hitting anyone.

Pull the rope to lift the sheet
high enough to get under.
Tie off the rope.

Spread out the corners of the sheet with
ropes tied to water bottles or buckets.

Make adjustments to get the tent as big as you want.

Made in the USA
Coppell, TX
15 January 2025

44054868R00021